CRIMSON
Love

CRIMSON
Love

MZ. RED

authorHOUSE®

AuthorHouse™
1663 Liberty Drive
Bloomington, IN 47403
www.authorhouse.com
Phone: 1-800-839-8640

Published by AuthorHouse   07/05/2012

ISBN: 978-1-4772-4003-8 (sc)
ISBN: 978-1-4772-4004-5 (e)

Library of Congress Control Number: 2012912245

Any people depicted in stock imagery provided by Thinkstock are models, and such images are being used for illustrative purposes only.
Certain stock imagery © Thinkstock.

This book is printed on acid-free paper.

Dedication

This book is dedicated to the—

Inspiration

Encouragement

Motivation

True Love and

Support that I received as I stepped out on the new path of my

journey . . . . Peace and much love to you . . .

&

To the mate of my soul . . . . Te Quiero . . .

Contents

Photography

I would like to give a "special" thank you to my photographer, "J.B".
Thanks for collaborating and capturing my vision, your photography is truly poetry on film.
Peace and Blessings to you and your family.

HEMA PHOTOS
THE BEHOLDER

Ibrahim and Muhubo Al-Qaabil
Freelance Photographer

Portraits, Wedding, Events, etc,

By Appointment Only
Phone: 301.467.5964
Email: hemaphotos11@gmail.com
http://www.wix.com/hemaphoto/hemaphotos
http://www.facebook.com/hemaphotography

http://www.wix.com/hemaphotos/hemaphotos

Mz. Red—Misread

Passionate—Fiery—Irrational
Bold-Beautiful-Sexy
Flips the Script
Plays to Her Audience
Smart-Polished-Urban
Big Heart-Loyal—Loving
Mz. Red—Misread

-Hop

Who Am I

I am one of a kind
I am a vanilla child filled with a chocolate soul
Been a R&B sista since some time ago
Always the black sheep of the family
Growing up, urban livin' has always been my scene
My friends were just my friends, never payin' attention
To the difference in our skin
Always a "fly girl",
That's right,
Asymetric hairdo,
Rockin' the lastest sneakers & hoop earrings too,
Actually, funny thing, I still do . . . .
Truly naïve to the "haters" that were in my surroundings
Obviously they were payin' more attention to my
"lightskinnedness",
Hanging in the urban scene, but no worries
I shook them all off a long, long time ago
Cause I am a vanilla child, filled with a chocolate soul
Now let me be clear and don't get it twisted . . .
I am not counterfeit, a copy, an imitation or a fraud
I know who I am and who God has destined for me to be,
From childhood to now,
This sista' got soul
Like nobody knows, that's for real,
I am a vanilla child,
Completely comfortable and confident
In this skin I'm in and
I am filled with a beautiful, sexy and full of love
Chocolate soul . . . .

New Womanhood

Born into sovereignty on a fall
afternoon,
in the outskirts between here and there
she emerged from a cocoon of confinement,
healing from deep wounds, heartache and pain
first breathe taken in a room of crimson and brown
that embraced her naked and exposed soul
first glimpse upon a sunlight horizon of pink and red hues
she stretched her beautiful new wings of freedom
found deep within her essence
empowered with new womanhood
new horizons, new visions, new breathe for life
and love
this beautiful new butterfly
can fiercely soar through this new journey
with a
rejuvenated Soul
vivacious Spirit
radiant Beauty
and loving Life . . .

A Conversation

Casual conversation
a friendly invitation
resting of one's heart
relaxation
freeing of one's mind
pleasantly surprised
by deep soulful thoughts
compassion shared
secrets told & intertwined
in the atmosphere
his lap, her pillow
stimulation
realization of kindred souls
embrace
his hand rests on the small
of her back
deep slumber
intimacy without
intimacy
true love passing
between their lips
ignited chemistry
sultriness burns from their skin
passion ensues
love making of the mind and soul
nothing can be more
beautiful
than an inviting
conversation . . .

Beautiful Three

Three beautiful strangers
drifted into my life,
so unexpectedly
surprisingly
three beautiful blessings
love me unconditionally
three beautiful angels
floated into my atmosphere
I gaze at them often
all three unique and exquisite
my beautiful three
seeds
I have poured
and planted pieces of my soul
for nourishment
within each of all three
Child one
Child two
Child three
are my legacy
my beautiful three
babies
I love them with all
my heart and
soul . . . .

Been . . . .

Been hurt throughout my life
Been up, been down
Been disowned for being different
Been the young, unwed mother
Been lied to, cheated on
Been married/divorced a time or two,
Been neglected, used and abused
Been drowning in sorrow
Been broken spiritually
Been mending my broken heart, clairvoyantly
Been contemplating a lot of thoughts running through my mind,
through my mind,
Been wondering how much more can one take,
especially when your heart and soul is crying out,
But please hear me, when I tell you
I fell on my hands and knees and cried out
Been prayin' to God for healin'
Been prayin' for deliverance
please hear me when I tell you
God answers prayers
Been prayin', I'm healed
Been prayin', I'm delivered
Been prayin', I'm blessed
Been prayin', I'm happy
Been prayin', I'm a survivor
Been prayin', I'm lovin' me
I'm walking in my destiny
I'm praisin' His name,
I'm thankful,
I'm livin' my dream,

Been prayin',
thank you Heavenly Father,
for lovin' and savin' me,
I made it because of you,
you lead me out of the darkness
into the light . . . .

Passages

Baby I've been
so unknowingly naive to you
all these years
that have passed
between us
blinded to your love
that's been in front of
me
you've been standing,
waiting,
reaching out for me
but in other directions
I traveled,
in the distant horizon you
called my name
but I never heard you
passages, many did you
write me,
but between the lines
I didn't see your waiting interest

Out of the blue
stopped destiny
to open my eyes to see you,
to set me on the right path
to you,

and I finally heard
you call my name
for the first time
in the essence of
genuine love
from the depth
of passages to and from your heart . . . .

Midnight bubble bath

Midnight bubble bath
candlelight ambience,
moonlit sky,
confessions flow from lovers
lips,
legs intertwined
their bodies melt into one
lovemaking ensues
her breasts pressed
against his chest
her thighs wrapped
around his chiseled waist
his manhood penetrating deep
within her essence
his hands firmly grasping
her backside
as their erotic movement
creates waves
crashing against a sandy shore
losing breath
intoxication
lips exploring
one another
eyes embrace
climatic explosion
exit the bubble bath
enter the bedroom
sexual pleasures
again,
again,
&
again . . . .

Brown Sugar Soul

There is a man,
I think I'll call him
Brown Sugar Soul
yeah that's him
he walked into my life
so unexpectedly
an operator of smooth
no doubt
he's definitely a smooth operator
that Brown Sugar Soul
rocks my mind up, my body down,
my soul left to right
that
Brown Sugar Soul
has the softest hands, muscular body
he has put moves on me like no other
he resuscitated my breath for life
he revives the intimate pulse of my womanhood
I am fallin' for him
I pour my soul into him
I am digging him, I mean, really feeling him
that Brown Sugar Soul
he is so sweet, sexy and has a big swagger for days,
Oooooowwwweeeeee, he leaves me speechless,
that Brown Sugar Soul
he raptures me from head to toe
he embraces me with his strong arms
he rubs my backside so tenderly
or better yet
should I call him

Downtown Sugar Brown
he travels downtown and dines on my red essence
damn, he's bringing my sexy back
That Brown Sugar Soul
is the very substance of a real man and
I love him so . . .

Inspired by You

Where did you come from,
I am in awe by you, enthralled by you,
I didn't see you coming
did you hear my thoughts . . . .
Did our planets align in the star filled sky
above

or

Are you my heaven sent angel that I
have prayed for all my life . . . .
my love,
where did you come from,
you have awoken a part of my inner being that
has been dormant for some time,
I'm so excited by you, you feel so right in my
spirit and soul,

yet,

I can't comprehend it
what took you so long to find your sweet
and rescue her from the journey to nowhere,
are you my soul mate, and it is now the season for our
souls to mate ?
You speak to me as if I have told you all
my innermost secrets,
I pinch myself to see if I am going to awake
from a deep slumber
where did you come from . . . .
I may never know,
but
what matters most is that you are here
and
I am yours . . .

Surrendered

Here
I am
in love
with you
Baby
my body
is naked
for you to
embrace
my heart
is
unguarded for your
love to takeover
my mind is
open
for you
to Inhabit
my soul is
revealed
for yours
to intertwine
my lips are
moist, wet and pouty
for you to kiss
my thickness, my round hips
are
for you to
be inspired,
to grasp,
to hold,

to caress,
you see baby
here I am in
love with you,
with all of
me
surrendered to you . . .

Glow

A new glow
encompasses my soul,
radiance is my reflection,
love dwells deeply within,
laughter inhabits my spirit
a new flavor refreshes my lips,
happiness is my halo,
healing is strengthening my broken
heart,
restoration runs through my veins
beauty and intrigue sparkles in my eyes
inspiration sways in my hips
I breathe in tranquility
peace is in my mind
renewal is the praise in my spirit
joy is my new sunrise
serenity is my new sunset
on my beautiful horizon
with a new glow . . .

The One

One touch
and I know
I belong to him
One look
and I know he
only has eyes for me
One smile
and I know I can't
resist
One word
and I know he
holds me captive
One embrace
and I know there is
no where else I'd rather be
One kiss
and I know the passion he has
for me
One confession
and I know his heart belongs
to me
One movement
and I know I am mesmerized
by how beautiful he walks
One man
and I know
I am the true
woman for him . . .

I can, You can't

Woke since 3:30 am
feeling feverish, body aches
running thoughts of
you
of us
through my mind
you ask me why I love you,
how can I love you?
and my response is
I can love you
cause you can't see the beautiful
man before me,
inside and out,
I can love you
cause you can't control
the way my heart skips
a beat whenever you're around
I can love you
cause you can't interfere with
fate and being the
true mate to my soul
I can love you
cause you can't
restrain how you feel about
me
I can love you
cause you can't
constrain the natural chemistry
between us
I can love you

cause baby you can't
erase the steps
of our intertwined
path paved
in love . . . .

He Gives Good Voice

Hey baby girl, says he
on the other end of the phone
I melt with every syllable
pronunciation
sound
he gives good voice
to me on a regular
I can't go a day
without
whether he's talking
business sophisticate, proper
or
round the way, what's up slang
the
underground intonation
that dwells deep within him
is soulful, penetrating, intoxicating
he gives good voice
to me on a regular my
own voice I will vacate
just to hear my baby
on the other
end of the
line say my name . . . .

Brown Sugar Soul/Remix

Brown, having the color of chocolate
Sugar, a sweet substance
Soul, his very essence

Chocolate sweet essence,
that's Brown Sugar Soul
tall, dark and handsome is he,
immaculately tailored
for the 9 to 5,
beautiful bald head,
shaped up beard,
dark brows,
smell good splashed all over his body . . .
But can be the sexy dress down in
his jeans and T,
Got a little bow legged goin' on,
I'm just saying, let me collect myself. . . .
ok, let's continue,
thought provoking
refreshingly profound
charismatic
honest
driven
heroic
but will break it down
for his red lady,
and give that shoulder to cry on
arms to hold me,
muscular chest to lay my head
and listen to that strong, soulful heart beat

like a congo drum
wow, it's playin' our song
his avenue of approach
his technique
will make me lose all self control
and forget my name
say my name, say my name
oh yeah, Mz. Red, right
don't let anyone tell you different,
Everything tastes better
With Brown Sugar . . . .

Take flight

Mate with my soul,
take flight with my
kindred spirit
through the star filled night
sky . . . .
our love will
continuously orbit planet
Neptune . . . .
You will always remain
Beautiful
to me . . . .

Love lines

Gray
line of love
engraved
in the palm of his hand
fiery red
Gypsy queen
ran across his path
by fate
his fortune she freely
read
he is her destined
Love
and with one touch,
one kiss of passion
his love line
began to beat
a pulse
no more gray matter
no flat lines
but streaks of red
has tattooed his
palm with
love . . . .

New flavor

Seasoned & Sexy,
my new flavor
his taste still lingers on my lips
Seasoned & Sexy,
makes me smile and laugh
like no other
Seasoned & Sexy,
makes love to my mind
and caresses my imperfections,
Seasoned & Sexy,
rocks my body and soul
all day and all night
oh so right,
Seasoned & Sexy,
makes me exhale
and kisses my tears away,
Seasoned & Sexy,
believe me age ain't
nothin' but a number,
Seasoned & Sexy,
I've got mine, girlfriend find
your own . . . .

Love, Feel, Breathe

This feeling of love between us two
I feel and breathe it
all in
so rare
is the love
so beautiful knowing
it exists
as it escapes
our hearts
spoken through our
ever embracing, sensuous, thick
lips
your touch
soothes me like
a calm after the storm,
you're so giving of every fiber
in your being which
makes my spirit soar
beyond the horizons
to catch a glimpse of
our dreams, our love, our actuality
how
beautiful
exquisite
enticing
our lives
will be, when
I catch my
breath
It's your love

I hear
Calling my name
in the atmosphere
I return
to
Love U, Feel U, Breathe U

Waiting

Here I stand,
in love,
never planned this,
never really knew after
all these years it would be
you,
my soul mate,
how beautiful is the love
we share,
it surrounds us everywhere
we go,
but complication set in,
you left to protect me,
us,
yet
I'm waiting for
you to return to be by
my side,
I still stand here more
in love than the day
before,

Author Bio

Karen Nock, aka: "Mz. Red", is on the rise to fulfill her lifelong dream of publishing her secret passion: Poetry. Mz. Red is a true Washingtonian at heart and raised in suburban Maryland. Mz. Red is a forty-two year old mother of three beautiful children, Britt, Ish and Dre'. Also, she is a grandmother/aka: "Gigi" to one adorable grandson, Chayce.

The woman known as "Mz. Red" is at times "Misread", but let's set the record straight, she is: A VIVACIOUS VIRGO, LOVING LIFE, SOULFUL, HUMOROUS, VERY HAPPY, SPIRITUAL, DEDICATED AND IN LOVE . . . .